FRACTIONS
SECOND GRADE
MATH ESSENTIALS

Children's Fraction Books

BOBO'S
LITTLE BRIANIAC BOOKS

educational & informative books for children
(PRE-K / K-12)

Fraction Exercises

Write the fraction of the shaded area.

1.) _____

2.) _____

3.) _____

4.) _____

5.)   _____

6.) _____

7.) _____

8.) _____

9.) _____

10.)   _____

Write the fraction of the shaded area.

1.) _____

2.) _____

3.) _____

4.) _____

5.) _____

6.) _____

7.) _____

8.) _____

9.) _____

10.) _____

Write the fraction of the shaded area.

1.)   _____

6.)   _____

2.)   _____

7.) 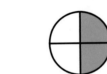   _____

3.)   _____

8.)   _____

4.)   _____

9.)   _____

5.)   _____

10.)   _____

Exercise No. 4

Write the fraction of the shaded area.

1.) _____

2.) _____

3.) _____

4.) _____

5.) _____

6.) _____

7.) _____

8.) _____

9.) _____

10.) _____

Exercise No. 5

Write the fraction of the shaded area.

1.) _____

2.) _____

3.) _____

4.) _____

5.) _____

6.) _____

7.) _____

8.) _____

9.) _____

10.) _____

Write the fraction of the shaded area.

1.) _____

2.) _____

3.) _____

4.) _____

5.) _____

6.) _____

7.) _____

8.) _____

9.) _____

10.) _____

Write the fraction of the shaded area.

1.)   _____

2.)   _____

3.)   _____

4.)   _____

5.)   _____

6.)   _____

7.)   _____

8.)   _____

9.)   _____

10.)   _____

Exercise No. 8

Write the fraction of the shaded area.

1.) _____

2.) _____

3.) _____

4.) _____

5.) _____

6.) _____

7.) _____

8.) _____

9.) _____

10.) _____

Exercise No. 9

Write the fraction of the shaded area.

1.) _____

2.) _____

3.) _____

4.) _____

5.) _____

6.) _____

7.) _____

8.) _____

9.)  _____

10.) _____

Write the fraction of the shaded area.

1.) _____

2.) _____

3.) _____

4.) _____

5.) _____

6.) _____

7.) _____

8.) _____

9.) _____

10.) _____

Exercise No. 11

Shade the Figure with the Indicated Fraction.

1.) $\dfrac{7}{8}$

2.) $\dfrac{1}{3}$

3.) $\dfrac{4}{5}$

4.) $\dfrac{3}{5}$

5.) $\dfrac{4}{5}$

6.) $\dfrac{1}{8}$

7.) $\dfrac{3}{4}$

8.) $\dfrac{3}{5}$

9.) $\dfrac{2}{5}$

10.) $\dfrac{1}{5}$

Shade the Figure with the Indicated Fraction.

1.) $\dfrac{2}{5}$

2.) $\dfrac{1}{4}$

3.) 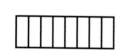 $\dfrac{5}{8}$

4.) $\dfrac{2}{4}$

5.)  $\dfrac{4}{8}$

6.) $\dfrac{2}{3}$

7.) $\dfrac{1}{2}$

8.) 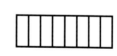 $\dfrac{6}{8}$

9.) 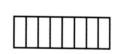 $\dfrac{3}{8}$

10.) 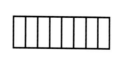 $\dfrac{2}{8}$

Exercise No. 13

Shade the Figure with the Indicated Fraction.

1.) $\dfrac{2}{8}$

2.) $\dfrac{2}{3}$

3.) $\dfrac{3}{4}$

4.) $\dfrac{4}{5}$

5.) $\dfrac{1}{2}$

6.) $\dfrac{1}{8}$

7.) $\dfrac{2}{5}$

8.) $\dfrac{6}{8}$

9.) $\dfrac{7}{8}$

10.)  $\dfrac{5}{8}$

Exercise No. 14

Shade the Figure with the Indicated Fraction.

1.) $\dfrac{2}{5}$

2.) $\dfrac{3}{5}$

3.) $\dfrac{3}{5}$

4.) 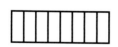 $\dfrac{4}{8}$

5.) $\dfrac{3}{8}$

6.) $\dfrac{1}{5}$

7.) $\dfrac{1}{4}$

8.) $\dfrac{4}{5}$

9.) $\dfrac{1}{3}$

10.) $\dfrac{2}{4}$

Exercise No. 15

Shade the Figure with the Indicated Fraction.

1.) $\dfrac{2}{4}$

2.) $\dfrac{3}{5}$

3.) $\dfrac{1}{8}$

4.) $\dfrac{3}{5}$

5.) $\dfrac{3}{4}$

6.) $\dfrac{6}{8}$

7.) $\dfrac{4}{5}$

8.)  $\dfrac{4}{5}$

9.)  $\dfrac{7}{8}$

10.) $\dfrac{2}{5}$

Exercise No. 16

Shade the Figure with the Indicated Fraction.

1.) $\dfrac{2}{5}$

2.) $\dfrac{2}{3}$

3.) $\dfrac{1}{3}$

4.) $\dfrac{1}{5}$

5.) $\dfrac{2}{8}$

6.) $\dfrac{1}{2}$

7.) $\dfrac{3}{8}$

8.)  $\dfrac{4}{8}$

9.) $\dfrac{1}{4}$

10.) $\dfrac{5}{8}$

Shade the Figure with the Indicated Fraction.

1.) $\dfrac{6}{8}$

2.) $\dfrac{1}{5}$

3.) $\dfrac{5}{8}$

4.) $\dfrac{4}{5}$

5.) $\dfrac{2}{4}$

6.) $\dfrac{2}{5}$

7.) $\dfrac{2}{8}$

8.) $\dfrac{1}{2}$

9.) $\dfrac{7}{8}$

10.) $\dfrac{4}{5}$

Shade the Figure with the Indicated Fraction.

1.) $\frac{3}{8}$

2.) $\frac{1}{4}$

3.) $\frac{1}{3}$

4.) $\frac{4}{8}$

5.) $\frac{3}{5}$

6.) $\frac{3}{4}$

7.) $\frac{2}{5}$

8.) $\frac{2}{3}$

9.) $\frac{3}{5}$

10.) $\frac{1}{8}$

Exercise No. 19

Shade the Figure with the Indicated Fraction.

1.) $\dfrac{3}{5}$

2.) $\dfrac{6}{8}$

3.) $\dfrac{1}{2}$

4.) $\dfrac{2}{8}$

5.) $\dfrac{2}{5}$

6.) $\dfrac{3}{4}$

7.) $\dfrac{2}{5}$

8.) $\dfrac{1}{5}$

9.) $\dfrac{5}{8}$

10.) $\dfrac{1}{3}$

Exercise No. 20

Shade the Figure with the Indicated Fraction.

1.) $\dfrac{3}{5}$ _____

2.) $\dfrac{4}{8}$ _____

3.) $\dfrac{4}{5}$ _____

4.) $\dfrac{1}{4}$ _____

5.) $\dfrac{3}{8}$ _____

6.) $\dfrac{7}{8}$ _____

7.) $\dfrac{1}{8}$ _____

8.) $\dfrac{4}{5}$ _____

9.) $\dfrac{2}{4}$ _____

10.) $\dfrac{2}{3}$ _____

Add the following fractions. Write and shade the correct answer.

1.) $\frac{5}{12}$ + $\frac{6}{12}$ = _____

2.) $\frac{2}{11}$ + $\frac{6}{11}$ = _____

3.) $\frac{2}{5}$ + $\frac{2}{5}$ = _____

4.) $\frac{1}{6}$ + $\frac{4}{6}$ = _____

5.) $\frac{4}{10}$ + $\frac{4}{10}$ = _____

6.) $\frac{2}{9}$ + $\frac{3}{9}$ = _____

7.) $\frac{2}{9}$ + $\frac{3}{9}$ = _____

8.) $\frac{2}{11}$ + $\frac{7}{11}$ = _____

9.) $\frac{1}{4}$ + $\frac{1}{4}$ = _____

10.) $\frac{2}{12}$ + $\frac{7}{12}$ = _____

Exercise No. 22

Add the following fractions. Write and shade the correct answer.

1.)

$\frac{2}{11} + \frac{4}{11} = $ _____

2.)

$\frac{1}{9} + \frac{1}{9} = $ _____

3.)

$\frac{2}{8} + \frac{3}{8} = $ _____

4.)

$\frac{2}{7} + \frac{2}{7} = $ _____

5.)

$\frac{2}{5} + \frac{2}{5} = $ _____

6.)

$\frac{2}{5} + \frac{2}{5} = $ _____

7.)

$\frac{1}{10} + \frac{8}{10} = $ _____

8.)

$\frac{2}{8} + \frac{3}{8} = $ _____

9.)

$\frac{1}{9} + \frac{5}{9} = $ _____

10.)

$\frac{4}{11} + \frac{6}{11} = $ _____

Exercise No. 23

Add the following fractions. Write and shade the correct answer.

1.)

$\dfrac{3}{9}$ + $\dfrac{5}{9}$ = _____

2.)

$\dfrac{2}{12}$ + $\dfrac{7}{12}$ = _____

3.)

$\dfrac{2}{11}$ + $\dfrac{8}{11}$ = _____

4.)

$\dfrac{2}{7}$ + $\dfrac{3}{7}$ = _____

5.)

$\dfrac{2}{10}$ + $\dfrac{2}{10}$ = _____

6.)

$\dfrac{1}{6}$ + $\dfrac{2}{6}$ = _____

7.)

$\dfrac{1}{5}$ + $\dfrac{3}{5}$ = _____

8.)

$\dfrac{4}{11}$ + $\dfrac{5}{11}$ = _____

9.)

$\dfrac{1}{12}$ + $\dfrac{6}{12}$ = _____

10.)

$\dfrac{3}{12}$ + $\dfrac{4}{12}$ = _____

Exercise No. 24

Add the following fractions. Write and shade the correct answer.

1.) $\frac{1}{11}$ + $\frac{1}{11}$ = _____

2.) $\frac{1}{6}$ + $\frac{4}{6}$ = _____

3.) $\frac{2}{7}$ + $\frac{4}{7}$ = _____

4.) $\frac{1}{8}$ + $\frac{6}{8}$ = _____

5.) $\frac{1}{6}$ + $\frac{3}{6}$ = _____

6.) $\frac{5}{12}$ + $\frac{6}{12}$ = _____

7.) $\frac{2}{11}$ + $\frac{6}{11}$ = _____

8.) $\frac{2}{12}$ + $\frac{9}{12}$ = _____

9.) $\frac{1}{6}$ + $\frac{4}{6}$ = _____

10.) $\frac{4}{10}$ + $\frac{4}{10}$ = _____

Exercise No. 25

Add the following fractions.

1.) $\dfrac{2}{11} + \dfrac{3}{11} =$

2.) $\dfrac{1}{10} + \dfrac{3}{10} =$

3.) $\dfrac{2}{6} + \dfrac{3}{6} =$

4.) $\dfrac{1}{3} + \dfrac{1}{3} =$

5.) $\dfrac{2}{9} + \dfrac{6}{9} =$

6.) $\dfrac{1}{10} + \dfrac{8}{10} =$

7.) $\dfrac{2}{8} + \dfrac{4}{8} =$

8.) $\dfrac{2}{11} + \dfrac{5}{11} =$

9.) $\dfrac{2}{9} + \dfrac{6}{9} =$

10.) $\dfrac{3}{12} + \dfrac{3}{12} =$

Add the following fractions.

1.) $\dfrac{2}{11} + \dfrac{8}{11} =$

2.) $\dfrac{2}{12} + \dfrac{6}{12} =$

3.) $\dfrac{3}{10} + \dfrac{6}{10} =$

4.) $\dfrac{3}{9} + \dfrac{4}{9} =$

5.) $\dfrac{1}{6} + \dfrac{3}{6} =$

6.) $\dfrac{1}{9} + \dfrac{1}{9} =$

7.) $\dfrac{1}{3} + \dfrac{1}{3} =$

8.) $\dfrac{3}{12} + \dfrac{5}{12} =$

9.) $\dfrac{2}{11} + \dfrac{6}{11} =$

10.) $\dfrac{1}{12} + \dfrac{7}{12} =$

Exercise No. 27

Add the following fractions.

1.) $\dfrac{1}{6} + \dfrac{4}{6} =$

2.) $\dfrac{2}{12} + \dfrac{7}{12} =$

3.) $\dfrac{1}{11} + \dfrac{5}{11} =$

4.) $\dfrac{1}{7} + \dfrac{3}{7} =$

5.) $\dfrac{2}{10} + \dfrac{7}{10} =$

6.) $\dfrac{2}{11} + \dfrac{7}{11} =$

7.) $\dfrac{1}{3} + \dfrac{1}{3} =$

8.) $\dfrac{1}{4} + \dfrac{1}{4} =$

9.) $\dfrac{3}{8} + \dfrac{4}{8} =$

10.) $\dfrac{2}{10} + \dfrac{6}{10} =$

Add the following fractions.

1.) $\dfrac{1}{5} + \dfrac{2}{5} =$

2.) $\dfrac{1}{3} + \dfrac{1}{3} =$

3.) $\dfrac{1}{11} + \dfrac{7}{11} =$

4.) $\dfrac{2}{12} + \dfrac{7}{12} =$

5.) $\dfrac{3}{12} + \dfrac{4}{12} =$

6.) $\dfrac{2}{6} + \dfrac{3}{6} =$

7.) $\dfrac{1}{11} + \dfrac{4}{11} =$

8.) $\dfrac{1}{4} + \dfrac{2}{4} =$

9.) $\dfrac{5}{12} + \dfrac{5}{12} =$

10.) $\dfrac{2}{10} + \dfrac{2}{10} =$

GOOD LUCK!

Answers

Exercise No. 1

1.) $\frac{1}{4}$

2.) $\frac{1}{5}$

3.) $\frac{6}{8}$

4.) $\frac{2}{3}$

5.) $\frac{4}{5}$

6.) $\frac{5}{8}$

7.) $\frac{3}{5}$

8.) $\frac{7}{8}$

9.) $\frac{2}{8}$

10.) $\frac{2}{4}$

Exercise No. 2

1.) $\frac{3}{5}$

2.) $\frac{3}{4}$

3.) $\frac{1}{2}$

4.) $\frac{1}{3}$

5.) $\frac{1}{8}$

6.) $\frac{4}{8}$

7.) $\frac{3}{8}$

8.) $\frac{2}{5}$

9.) $\frac{4}{5}$

10.) $\frac{2}{5}$

Exercise No. 3

1.) $\frac{3}{5}$

2.) $\frac{1}{8}$

3.) $\frac{3}{5}$

4.) $\frac{5}{8}$

5.) $\frac{2}{8}$

6.) $\frac{3}{8}$

7.) $\frac{2}{4}$

8.) $\frac{1}{3}$

9.) $\frac{2}{5}$

10.) $\frac{2}{3}$

Exercise No. 4

1.) $\frac{1}{2}$

2.) $\frac{2}{5}$

3.) $\frac{4}{5}$

4.) $\frac{6}{8}$

5.) $\frac{1}{4}$

6.) $\frac{3}{4}$

7.) $\frac{7}{8}$

8.) $\frac{4}{5}$

9.) $\frac{1}{5}$

10.) $\frac{4}{8}$

Answers

Exercise No. 5

1.) $\frac{3}{5}$

2.) $\frac{5}{8}$

3.) $\frac{2}{5}$

4.) $\frac{4}{5}$

5.) $\frac{2}{8}$

6.) $\frac{3}{8}$

7.) $\frac{2}{3}$

8.) $\frac{2}{5}$

9.) $\frac{6}{8}$

10.) $\frac{4}{5}$

Exercise No. 6

1.) $\frac{1}{3}$

2.) $\frac{4}{8}$

3.) $\frac{3}{4}$

4.) $\frac{1}{5}$

5.) $\frac{1}{4}$

6.) $\frac{2}{4}$

7.) $\frac{1}{2}$

8.) $\frac{7}{8}$

9.) $\frac{1}{8}$

10.) $\frac{3}{5}$

Exercise No. 7

1.) $\frac{3}{8}$

2.) $\frac{4}{8}$

3.) $\frac{6}{8}$

4.) $\frac{1}{5}$

5.) $\frac{1}{2}$

6.) $\frac{5}{8}$

7.) $\frac{1}{8}$

8.) $\frac{4}{5}$

9.) $\frac{2}{8}$

10.) $\frac{3}{4}$

Exercise No. 8

1.) $\frac{2}{5}$

2.) $\frac{1}{4}$

3.) $\frac{1}{3}$

4.) $\frac{2}{5}$

5.) $\frac{2}{4}$

6.) $\frac{2}{3}$

7.) $\frac{3}{5}$

8.) $\frac{7}{8}$

9.) $\frac{4}{5}$

10.) $\frac{3}{5}$

Answers

Exercise No. 9

1.) $\dfrac{7}{8}$

2.) $\dfrac{2}{8}$

3.) $\dfrac{4}{8}$

4.) $\dfrac{2}{3}$

5.) $\dfrac{1}{8}$

6.) $\dfrac{4}{5}$

7.) $\dfrac{5}{8}$

8.) $\dfrac{1}{3}$

9.) $\dfrac{3}{4}$

10.) $\dfrac{1}{2}$

Exercise No. 10

1.) $\dfrac{3}{8}$

2.) $\dfrac{2}{4}$

3.) $\dfrac{1}{5}$

4.) $\dfrac{1}{4}$

5.) $\dfrac{6}{8}$

6.) $\dfrac{3}{5}$

7.) $\dfrac{3}{5}$

8.) $\dfrac{4}{5}$

9.) $\dfrac{2}{5}$

10.) $\dfrac{2}{5}$

Exercise No. 11

1.)  $\dfrac{7}{8}$

2.) $\dfrac{1}{3}$

3.) $\dfrac{4}{5}$

4.) $\dfrac{3}{5}$

5.) $\dfrac{4}{5}$

6.) $\dfrac{1}{8}$

7.) $\dfrac{3}{4}$

8.) $\dfrac{3}{5}$

9.) $\dfrac{2}{5}$

10.) $\dfrac{1}{5}$

Exercise No. 12

1.) $\dfrac{2}{5}$

2.) $\dfrac{1}{4}$

3.) $\dfrac{5}{8}$

4.) $\dfrac{2}{4}$

5.) $\dfrac{4}{8}$

6.) $\dfrac{2}{3}$

7.) $\dfrac{1}{2}$

8.) $\dfrac{6}{8}$

9.) $\dfrac{3}{8}$

10.) $\dfrac{2}{8}$

Answers

Exercise No. 13

1 $\dfrac{2}{8}$

6.) $\dfrac{1}{8}$

2 $\dfrac{2}{3}$

7.) $\dfrac{2}{5}$

3 $\dfrac{3}{4}$

8.) $\dfrac{6}{8}$

4 $\dfrac{4}{5}$

9.) $\dfrac{7}{8}$

5 $\dfrac{1}{2}$

10.) $\dfrac{5}{8}$

Exercise No. 14

1.) $\dfrac{2}{5}$

6.) $\dfrac{1}{5}$

2.) $\dfrac{3}{5}$

7.) $\dfrac{1}{4}$

3.) $\dfrac{3}{5}$

8.) $\dfrac{4}{5}$

4.) $\dfrac{4}{8}$

9.) $\dfrac{1}{3}$

5.)  $\dfrac{3}{8}$

10.)  $\dfrac{2}{4}$

Exercise No. 15

1.) $\dfrac{2}{4}$

6.) $\dfrac{6}{8}$

2.) $\dfrac{3}{5}$

7.) $\dfrac{4}{5}$

3.) $\dfrac{1}{8}$

8.) $\dfrac{4}{5}$

4.) $\dfrac{3}{5}$

9.) $\dfrac{7}{8}$

5.) $\dfrac{3}{4}$

10.) $\dfrac{2}{5}$

Exercise No. 16

1.) $\dfrac{2}{5}$

6.) $\dfrac{1}{2}$

2.) $\dfrac{2}{3}$

7.) $\dfrac{3}{8}$

3.) $\dfrac{1}{3}$

8.) $\dfrac{4}{8}$

4.) $\dfrac{1}{5}$

9.) $\dfrac{1}{4}$

5.) $\dfrac{2}{8}$

10.) $\dfrac{5}{8}$

Answers

Exercise No. 17

1.) $\dfrac{6}{8}$

2.) $\dfrac{1}{5}$

3.) $\dfrac{5}{8}$

4.) $\dfrac{4}{5}$

5.) $\dfrac{2}{4}$

6.) $\dfrac{2}{5}$

7.) $\dfrac{2}{8}$

8.) $\dfrac{1}{2}$

9.) $\dfrac{7}{8}$

10.) $\dfrac{4}{5}$

Exercise No. 18

1.) 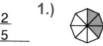 $\dfrac{3}{8}$

2.) 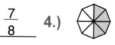 $\dfrac{1}{4}$

3.) $\dfrac{1}{3}$

4.) $\dfrac{4}{8}$

5.) $\dfrac{3}{5}$

6.) $\dfrac{3}{4}$

7.) $\dfrac{2}{5}$

8.) $\dfrac{2}{3}$

9.) $\dfrac{3}{5}$

10. $\dfrac{1}{8}$

Exercise No. 19

1.) $\dfrac{3}{5}$

2.) $\dfrac{6}{8}$

3.) $\dfrac{1}{2}$

4.) $\dfrac{2}{8}$

5.) $\dfrac{2}{5}$

6.) $\dfrac{3}{4}$

7.) $\dfrac{2}{5}$

8.) $\dfrac{1}{5}$

9.) $\dfrac{5}{8}$

10.) $\dfrac{1}{3}$

Exercise No. 20

1.) $\dfrac{3}{5}$

2.) $\dfrac{4}{8}$

3.) $\dfrac{4}{5}$

4.) $\dfrac{1}{4}$

5.) $\dfrac{3}{8}$

6.) $\dfrac{4}{8}$

7.) $\dfrac{2}{3}$

8.) $\dfrac{2}{5}$

9.) $\dfrac{5}{8}$

10.) $\dfrac{1}{2}$

Answers

Exercise No. 21

1.) $\frac{11}{12}$

2.) $\frac{8}{11}$

3.) $\frac{4}{5}$

4.) $\frac{5}{6}$

5.) $\frac{8}{10}$

6.) $\frac{5}{9}$

7.) $\frac{5}{9}$

8.) $\frac{9}{11}$

9.) $\frac{2}{4}$

10.) $\frac{9}{12}$

Exercise No. 22

1.) $\frac{6}{11}$

2.) $\frac{2}{9}$

3.) $\frac{5}{8}$

4.) $\frac{4}{7}$

5.) $\frac{4}{5}$

6.) $\frac{4}{5}$

7.) $\frac{9}{10}$

8.) $\frac{5}{8}$

9.) $\frac{6}{9}$

10.) $\frac{10}{11}$

Exercise No. 23

1.) $\frac{8}{9}$

2.) $\frac{9}{12}$

3.) $\frac{2}{3}$

4.) $\frac{5}{7}$

5.) $\frac{4}{10}$

6.) $\frac{3}{6}$

7.) $\frac{4}{5}$

8.) $\frac{9}{11}$

9.) $\frac{7}{12}$

10.) $\frac{7}{12}$

Exercise No. 24

1.) $\frac{2}{11}$

2.) $\frac{5}{6}$

3.) $\frac{9}{10}$

4.) $\frac{3}{5}$

5.) $\frac{3}{4}$

6.) $\frac{3}{9}$

7.) $\frac{8}{9}$

8.) $\frac{9}{10}$

9.) $\frac{5}{6}$

10.) $\frac{5}{7}$

Answers

Exercise No. 25

1.) $\dfrac{5}{6}$

2.) $\dfrac{9}{12}$

3.) $\dfrac{6}{11}$

4.) $\dfrac{4}{7}$

5.) $\dfrac{9}{10}$

6.) $\dfrac{9}{11}$

7.) $\dfrac{2}{3}$

8.) $\dfrac{2}{4}$

9.) $\dfrac{7}{8}$

10.) $\dfrac{8}{10}$

Exercise No. 26

1.) $\dfrac{10}{11}$

2.) $\dfrac{8}{12}$

3.) $\dfrac{9}{10}$

4.) $\dfrac{7}{9}$

5.) $\dfrac{4}{6}$

6.) $\dfrac{2}{9}$

7.) $\dfrac{2}{3}$

8.) $\dfrac{8}{12}$

9.) $\dfrac{8}{11}$

10.) $\dfrac{8}{12}$

Exercise No. 27

1.) $\dfrac{3}{5}$

2.) $\dfrac{2}{3}$

3.) $\dfrac{8}{11}$

4.) $\dfrac{9}{12}$

5.) $\dfrac{7}{12}$

6.) $\dfrac{5}{6}$

7.) $\dfrac{5}{11}$

8.) $\dfrac{3}{4}$

9.) $\dfrac{10}{12}$

10.) $\dfrac{4}{10}$

Exercise No. 28

1.) $\dfrac{3}{5}$

2.) $\dfrac{2}{3}$

3.) $\dfrac{8}{11}$

4.) $\dfrac{9}{12}$

5.) $\dfrac{7}{12}$

6.) $\dfrac{5}{6}$

7.) $\dfrac{5}{11}$

8.) $\dfrac{3}{4}$

9.) $\dfrac{10}{12}$

10.) $\dfrac{4}{10}$

35098238R00026

Made in the USA
Lexington, KY
31 March 2019